10 Secrets to
Straight A's

10 Secrets to Straight A's

How to Get Good Grades in School and Life

Brian Atchison

COLLEGE EDITION

Library of Congress Control Number
2016915152

ISBN 978-0-692-57636-6 (Stanford & Brooks)
ISBN 0692576363

Leanne Salandro, Designer
Editorial Review: Gina Vild, Cathlin Atchison

FIRST EDITION

10 9 8 7 6 5 4 3 2 1

Stanford & Brooks Publishers
Incline Village, NV

For My Children

*The future belongs to those who believe
in the beauty of their dreams.*

— Eleanor Roosevelt[1]

Forward

This reflects an updated edition of *The Secret to Straight A's*. It was originally written for my children, the most precious gifts in the world. I initially embarked on this project for my eldest daughter, who struggled with a demanding curriculum, and persevered day after day, and night after night—I am spectacularly proud of her.

Most schools, particularly the parochial ones she attended, ask a lot from our kids. I wanted her to succeed, but I didn't want her to do so at the expense of her childhood. So I wrote down the most important aspects of my own study experiences in the hope of helping her achieve even greater academic success than I have enjoyed. Isn't that what we all want for our children?

This book is geared toward college and college-bound high school students. It contains refinements that have benefited my two younger children. The first edition was aimed specifically toward children and supportive parents who wanted to inspire their children along the path of success.

My wish is for all who read this to gain the benefits that I garnered from "breaking the code." I want them to find peace from not having to struggle in school, to overcome that nagging dread that visited me often in my early school days when I wasn't prepared, didn't understand, or didn't have my homework. I want them to find the joy in learning.

Your best times in school are now! Enjoy and have fun!

Cheers,
Brian Atchison

OUTLINE

STEP 1   Find Your Motivation

STEP 2   Set Your Goals

STEP 3   Reward Yourself

STEP 4   Visualize Achievement

STEP 5   Use Affirmations

STEP 6   Organization and Time Management
(Or A Little Pressure is a Good Thing!)

Structure and Time-Setting
Preview Materials
Planning
Procrastination

STEP 7   Teacher Rapport

Live as if you were to die tomorrow.
Learn as if you were to live forever.

— Mahatma Gandhi[2]

Let's Begin, but first a story....

If someone had told me these simple things years ago, I would have been so much further ahead, but I'm grateful that I discovered them—eventually!

As a child I didn't like school. Let me be completely frank. I hated it with a passion! I attended a strict, parochial school, where—I believed—teachers were more skilled in the art of child-warfare than in the compassionate enterprise of teaching. To this day, I can clearly recall my fear when one of my teachers paced up and down the rows of desks while we were hard at work. The menacing jangle of wooden beads from her over-sized rosary hung like a cat-o-nine-tails from her waistband. I can still recall the smell of her starched habit wafting up and down the aisles—and when she stopped, it lingered in the air—a warning alarm that she was hovering behind me, scrutinizing my every move, waiting for a mistake, which—under the pressure—I invariably provided her.

It was a challenging introduction to education, and after that I was never comfortable in school until I went to college. It was then that I decided to make a study of studying. To figure out what separates the successful student from the one with potential, to finally *break the code.* And I did! I found these secrets not only served me well in school, but also in the many endeavors that followed, as I will explain later.

I should first give a bit of background and my bona fides. I was an average student in grammar school, and essentially a B student in high school. I didn't appreciate the importance of good grades at that age, nor did I realize how easily I could become an A student.

I remember the moment I decided to become a better student; NO! I remember the moment I decided to become an "A" student! It was at my high school graduation. The warm promise of summer filled the air. I was sitting in the outdoor audience with my class, cracking jokes, being funny. I was detached from the ceremony. I thought to myself, *let's get this over with!* My fog lifted when several of my friends and contemporaries began climbing the dais as their names were called to claim various academic awards and scholarships. I remember saying to myself, *where did these come from? What have I been doing with my time? I can do that, too!* It bothered me—a lot!

It was from that moment that I dedicated myself to uncovering the secrets of high academic achievement. What I didn't realize at the time, were the innumerable benefits to all areas of my life that would follow upon this discovery.

I learned that not only were A's achievable, but also that I could have them with less effort and time spent than it had taken me to achieve B's. Amazingly, I was happier, less stressed and had more free time. It's true! Even more, I was now in college and able to work before and after school to pay for my tuition and all of my flight training.

My dream was to become an airline pilot, but the expense of training was quite high, so I had to work, not only for my tuition and housing, but also for my flight training. Had I not discovered the keys to getting straight A's, I would never have been able to pursue, nor achieve, my true passion—flying for a living.

Why can I stand on my experience? I achieved it all. I graduated at the top of my class in the School of Engineering, Department of Aeronautics. I graduated with *Great Distinction*[3], and was even granted a scholarship from a major airline—*now I was standing on the dais!*

It took me almost a year to get my Private Pilot's License while a student in high school. I could only afford to pay for my lessons as I earned the money, but eventually I was able to get the initial certificate. In college I realized that to get further ratings, I would have to work smarter and faster, because in aviation time is money. All of my subsequent ratings were earned with minimum formal schooling. Most students take formal courses which prepare them for their tests. I would study and pass the written tests on my own. I embarked on my aviation education at the same time and in addition to my regular studies while attending college full time. I would then prepare myself for the practical tests using the techniques I developed in pursuit of academic excellence. My advanced ratings were achieved in days and weeks rather than months and years!

I share this with others, and they are amazed at such condensed timeframes, but I had gained the keys to academic success. I was getting faster and better as time went on. Each of the aeronautical ratings requires a written test of several hours as well as a practical exam in an airplane with an examiner; this is after acquiring myriad flight hours and compulsory instruction and before being allowed to take the practical exam.

In college I determined that I had to get out as soon as possible, so rather than attend classes I took advantage of the little-known opportunity to "challenge" a half a year of course-work. I did this without attending a single class. I passed every one that I attempted, graduating with a 3.85 overall average. This is when I realized that I had found the keys to academic success.

Did I achieve my dream? Yes! Today I am a Boeing 777 captain for one of the largest airlines in the world.

I will share with you what I've learned, but because it is so amazingly simple you won't believe it at first—that is until you put it into practice in your own life.

This is now the newly revised version. I would like you to benefit from an update to the above. Now we can look back a bit and see if these methods really work. Let me bring you up-to-date. My oldest child has now graduated from college and is enjoying a career in digital marketing. She won a scholarship for college at a renowned university and now works in a fast-growing area of business. I am so proud of her achievements and of the independent person she has become.

My second child, using my methods, has graduated from a prestigious university and enjoyed a Presidential scholarship while also working part-time. Throughout his college years he also worked for two U.S. Senators and graduated in 3.5 years with a perfect 4.0 (straight-A) average. Today he attends one of the top law schools in the country.

My youngest child has really benefited from the refinements we made over the years. She is open to self-improvement—and a risk taker. She lobbied the dean, the school president and even her mother while in high school in order to concurrently take Spanish and French languages. One semester she did the unthinkable and added an experimental Mandarin language program to Spanish and French. Three languages at the same time! She achieved top grades in all three. Presently she is a junior at one of the most sought after (and coolest) universities in the country. During her first two years she surfed almost every day and still earned a near perfect GPA—maintaining a scholarship.

I thought all of that was amazing enough, but she continues to surprise me. She made a mistake by not enrolling in a language course her first quarter, later discovering that she could not enroll in beginning Arabic until the next year, rather than the next quarter. This was unacceptable to her so she petitioned the department head, found a student in the class to tutor her and obtained the course materials, which she used to challenge first quarter Arabic. She passed and moved into second quarter Arabic with the rest of the students. After taking summer school classes in Washington D.C. as a beginning sophomore, she had already achieved third year level Arabic. She speaks four languages, and she learned only one of them at home!

She currently resides in the Middle East where she is advancing her Arabic studies and is conversational in two Arabic dialects in addition to Modern Standard Arabic.

As a parent, I could not be more proud of my children as students and as human beings. As one who has studied learning techniques, I am confident the methods I put forth are both uncomplicated and proven. They are honed to their essence—no fat here! They are just simple methods and techniques for gaining an advantage in today's most competitive academic landscape. Yet, it doesn't stop there. These concepts can be applied to success beyond academics. Take them out into the world and continue to enjoy your success into your future.

STEP 1

Find Your Motivation

Motivation will almost always beat mere talent.

— Norman R. Augustine[4]

The first step—and it has to be the first step—is to find motivation. I was motivated when I saw my classmates, most of whom I thought less gifted than I, taking home all of these awards and scholarships at my high school graduation. I was further motivated when I learned that less than one percent of the population become airline pilots. I believed that if I achieved academic excellence it would give me a leg up on the stiffest competition.

To find your motivation, do some soul searching. Give it some time. If it isn't already apparent, you might try sitting down and figuring out where you want to be in five and ten years. How do you picture yourself? What sort of job are you doing? What skills do you have? If you still can't figure this out, I recommend going to a guidance counselor at school, or at a local college, and ask to be evaluated for the kind of occupation to which your disposition is best suited.

I asked people in business what they like about what they do, and how they got to where they are. Do not be afraid to ask such questions of people in business, or the professions, as most people enjoy sharing their experiences, and they admire someone who is taking steps to achieve their goals. Remember, people like to help. If you are uncertain, I would advise exploring internships in areas in which you have an interest.

First and importantly, identify your goal and go for it! Conventional wisdom says:

Without a rudder,
even a fast ship will not get you to your destination.

STEP 2

Set Your Goals

Your goals, minus your doubts, equal your reality.

— Ralph Marston[5]

This doesn't sound important, but it is critical. Goal setting is probably two-thirds of the achievement battle. In goal setting you need short and long-term goals, and then you need to fine tune each goal with sub goals. Truly, it's not really complicated. Let me give you an example.

My goal was to be an airline pilot. Very concrete, that's good, but in need of intermediary goals to be achievable. A football team has a goal to win the game, but that isn't their only goal, but merely their ultimate goal. It requires interim steps, for example:

They need to:

1. **Goal 1: Score**
   a. Get hold of the ball.
   b. Get a first down.
   c. Get a touchdown
   d. Get the extra point

2. **Goal 2: Keep opposition from scoring**
   a. Prevent first down
      1. Pressure the Quarterback
      2. Keep rushing to a minimum

As you know, winning the game is the over-arching goal, but it requires several sub-goals to achieve. Do you get the big picture? If so, then fill in the interim goals.

An even better analogy is a road trip. I want to go from San Francisco to New York. Well, I can't just hop in my car and go. I'll not know the best way. I may not properly plan for gas and will end up stuck in the Nevada desert – or I'll be tired and not near a hotel to stop and rest. The entire excursion needs a plan with sub goals to define and achieve.

A significant step in achievement is:

Write down your goals

These should be honed down to clearly stated objectives. And in order to be effective they must contain another key ingredient.

Place a time next to each goal

You must give a time frame to each goal or your mind will not know when you must achieve it, and, hence, it becomes essentially unattainable.

Here is a goal:
    I will achieve ten pull-ups

Here is an attainable goal:
    I will achieve ten pull-ups in four weeks by
    January 16.

This tells your mind where you are relative to your timeline, and, if you need to increase your efforts or if you are ahead of schedule, maybe you can move your goal's time element forward. For example, you can plan to add one extra pull up a week, an achievable objective.

STEP 3

Reward Yourself

Self-reliance is the only road to true freedom,
and being one's own person is its ultimate reward.

— Patricia Sampson[6]

I remember my junior year in college. My sister was living in Lake Tahoe and offered me a place to stay anytime. I bought a season pass and arranged my classes so that I had Friday's free. This meant that in order to ski, I had to get ALL of my homework done by Thursday night. The thought of skiing three days made me race through my work during the week. It was a beautiful year.

Now this is the fun part. In order to achieve, you must give yourself a reward. Rewards are both large and small, like your goals, of course.

By example: You desire an A in chemistry. You state your goal: Achieve an A in Chem-1A this semester.

Now you set your reward so that you will have an incentive to achieve the goal. How about, "When I achieve this A, I will give myself a weekend at the beach." I would write this down, and I might even put a picture of the beach on my desk, and let my mind wander, picturing myself relaxing there.

Major goals deserve major rewards. The converse is also true: small goals deserve small rewards. An example might be: Get through a study period of two hours in preparation for a test or assignments. Reward: workout at the gym, go to a movie or call your girlfriend. The reward might also be as small as, "I'll get up and stretch after two more pages, or I'll get a glass of water at the end of this chapter." But remember, no reward until the goal is achieved. Eventually this system will become part of your routine.

You can really get performance out of yourself if you keep improving the challenge. Enhance the reward if the speed is picked up: "If I finish in an hour and a half, then I will see a movie AND buy an ice cream as well."

So remember, set a goal, set a reward, and don't allow yourself to enjoy the reward until you have had an achievement.

STEP 4

Visualize Achievement

Whatever you can do or dream you can, begin it.
Boldness has genius, power, and magic in it.
— Johann Wolfgang von Goethe[7]

Visualization is a key factor in achieving anything. It is the play in your head that you run over and over, refining it as you go. You are the lead. Visualize your way to success.

As an aspiring A-student, visualize yourself bringing home your report card. Everyone is amazed at your transformation. You drop it in the lap of your parents and say, "Now who is underachieving?" I recommend you do this to please yourself, but it is important to find out how you want the play to go, and keep playing it out in your head.

Why not try it now? Take a moment and visualize yourself as an A-student. How does that look to you? Who is there? Where are you standing when you are basking in your success? What are people saying to you, and what are you saying to them? Think it, and you can achieve it!

Once you discover how easy it is to achieve your A, you'll be able to apply these techniques to other goals in your life. Maybe you want to be a volleyball star. Visualize yourself in a game where you are performing at peak, where you are digging and spiking with ease. Visualization is a powerful tool. Figure out the outcome you most desire, and write the play in your head.

You might even try making a copy of your report card and filling in the A's yourself. Place it on your desk to keep it at the forefront of your thoughts. Visualize yourself getting your test back with an A firmly stamped on the front. Picture yourself effortlessly breezing through the exam with plenty of time left over to check your answers. You see yourself relaxed, enjoying the experience the test provides to show your knowledge. This is significant.

When I was in grammar school I always feared test day. I hated the lead up of fear. I hated being in the test room. I choked with fear when I should have been dashing off answers. That all changed when I arrived prepared. It is important to prepare yourself both academically and mentally. I taught myself how to actually—and I know you will roll your eyes, but it's true—look forward to the test. And more importantly, teach yourself how to relax during the test itself. What a difference that made!

Let me give you an example of how I used this technique in my flight training. I like to put a little pressure on myself. At the time, I was a flight instructor at the small airport where I learned to fly and I was seeking an opportunity to increase my flight experience. I was able to get through to the chief pilot of a small commuter airline in Ohio that was two thousand miles away. He told me interviews were being held the following Monday. He said that the candidates would be given an interview and evaluation class, with the successful ones to be hired right then. He said I was welcome to come and interview, but he made no promises.

"You do have your multi-engine rating don't you?" he asked.

"Of course," I answered.

Well, I didn't have the rating, but I had a few days to get it. Here is what I did. I called around to find a flight school that would allow me to gain accelerated training. This was Friday. I scheduled it for the next day. I showed up ready to work. Off we went to learn emergency procedures in an old Apache twin. I was shown all of the drills and then we went in for lunch. While we ate, I visualized all of the maneuvers. After lunch we went up again to conclude my training. We found an examiner who would give me my practical test the next day. I arrived at the airport early, sat in the airplane parked on the ramp and went through my visualizations, imagining the emergencies one after the other, letting my hands move over the controls as I sat in the seat. It was as good as a simulator ride. I passed the test easily with only 3.3 hours of total multi-engine time for the entire experience, both training and testing. Ironically, I didn't even have enough experience to rent the aircraft where I took the training, as their insurance required ten hours of multi-engine time logged.

No worries, I was going to get a flying job anyway. Actually, I quit my job that week as a flight instructor, took most of my money and put it down on a new car which could make the trip to Ohio, packed it with all of my worldly possessions—stereo and clothes—and headed east. I had burned the bridge behind me. There was no turning back. I really enjoyed the excitement of having no options, and believe me, your focus becomes razor sharp when you're working without a net. The rest of this story is even more exciting, but the point here is that visualization allowed me to succeed without spending money and time for actual training. Now this is an extreme example, but the principle applies to schoolwork as well...which brings me to my next point.

STEP 5

Use Affirmations

To achieve the marvelous,
it is precisely the unthinkable that must be thought.

— Tom Robbins, *Jitterbug Perfume*[8]

This is a secret weapon. Seriously, this is powerful, mind-bending stuff. High-achieving business leaders have spent millions of dollars on this. Don't dismiss it as theoretical. It is real.

What are affirmations? They are the little positive things we say to ourselves throughout the day, or at several intervals, which you set aside each day. An affirmation is defined as, "a positive assertion." Today you may see its use under a program called Neuro Linguistic Programming (NLP). You need to develop your own affirmations, and then write them down.

This is a very powerful tool to advance any objective. It employs the subconscious mind's <u>in</u>ability to make judgments, and only accept information it's given. Now what does this really mean, and how does this affect you?

Well, if you tell the subconscious mind —as in hypnosis—it will then accept something without the usual defenses and suspicion that our conscious mind uses to filter information. This is so critical to a healthy life that I cannot sufficiently emphasize its importance. After you see a few examples, come back and reread this section in order to appreciate the significance.

Some people go around with a dialogue in their heads saying things like, "I'm such a screw-up, and can never get things right. I'm such an idiot, how can I be so stupid?!" or, "I'm lousy at math; I don't have the mind for it. It's not my thing." Or, "I never do well on tests." Or, "I'm just not an 'A' student!"

Your subconscious hears this, and accepts it without judgment, without complaint—and then makes it your reality. Yes, the power is a double-edged sword, it can hurt as much as help, so don't misuse it, *ever.*

How do I employ affirmations?

It's so easy that you will be tempted to dismiss it as nonsense, but I caution you not to. The theory has been validated by numerous studies on achievement—affirmations are a large component, along with visualization of success.

When you develop your own affirmations, you must phrase them in only positive terms. Negative framing, or even negative wording, won't work. Here is a *bad* example:

"I will not get bad grades anymore."

Use Only Present Tense Affirmations.

There are several things wrong with this affirmation. First, it is future tense. Affirmations are most effective when couched in the present tense. Your subconscious will then accept this as your reality.

Do Not Use Negatives in Affirmations.

Second, the affirmation is full of both negativity and negative words. This affirmation implies that you are currently getting bad grades. The words "will not" will *not* register with your subconscious. It cannot process words such as "not, no, won't, never and the like.

So a good affirmation is cogent and stated positively in the present tense:

"I am a good student, because I enjoy learning new things."

"Each day I get better and better at schoolwork, because it is becoming easier and easier."

"I enjoy school."

"I enjoy tests and remain relaxed because they give me the opportunity to show how much I've learned."

"Tests are fun, I do well on tests."

"School is fun because I effortlessly find the important elements in each subject and remember them."

"I remember facts easily because I have a good imagination."

"I like to learn new things."

"I like to figure things out for myself."

"I am an A student."

"I enjoy math, it is simple and understandable."

"I'm getting better and faster at math each day—math is fun!"

"School is a game; I enjoy getting better at winning each day"

These are good affirmations. They are stated in the **present tense**, they are **positive** and they are **short**.

Now you probably look at these and say to yourself, "I don't believe them. I hate tests." Well, luckily that is not important. Your subconscious will believe the affirmations. Remember, it makes no judgment. If you read and repeat these throughout the day, they will become your reality, whether your conscious mind believes them or not. Let me say this again, it is important: You do not have to believe these affirmations when you develop them, they *will* become your reality over time, because your subconscious *will* believe them as written.

So carefully construct your own affirmations, perhaps five or ten at most to begin. Repeat them at least four times per day. More is better. *Important*: If you catch yourself saying, "I can't do this," or "I'm not good at that," or any other negative sentiment—get it out of your life. Be aware of this. Frankly, I was uncomfortable even writing the negative thoughts above because I was concerned my subconscious would accept them. Replace negative thoughts with positive ones until the negative thoughts are gone.

I encourage my children to get rid of negative things like, "I can't do this", or "I'm not good at that." If I hear anything like this, I bring it to their attention on the spot. But some people keep these thoughts in their heads and must be encouraged to eliminate them—you should eliminate them too.

Extra Credit:

Make a Worksheet for your goals. Here are some ideas.

If you have a copy of your report card, great! If not, make one up and place next to each subject the grade you want. This sounds silly, but the act of doing this will commit your goal to your mind's eye.

Now identify the subjects with which you have had difficulty. Determine what you find most difficult about them. Write a brief list of difficulties for each; take these and turn them into positive affirmations. Remember, no negative comments. Then be sure to throw away the list with your areas of difficulty, replace it with your positive affirmations. Hone them to short, powerful statements. This is well worth the trouble.

STEP 6

Organization and Time Management

(*Or: A Little Pressure is a Good Thing*)

*Time is at once the most valuable
and most perishable of all our possessions.*

— John Randolph[9]

Organize and Set Times

Before sitting down to do your work, organize it. I
recommend you do the most difficult subjects first while
you are fresh. If you have the option, it is advantageous
to determine when you are at your best for studying. I
found my peak studying time is before 11:00 am so I
structured my major study periods in the morning.

Your desk should be free of clutter. A cluttered desk
offers too many distractions. A clean one offers clarity. It
really is that simple.

To organize your work, set your books out in order of
their use. Make certain you have pens and paper,
reference books or whatever else you need at hand.
Don't keep getting up to gather these items as you work
because; it interrupts your progress—do it all
beforehand.

Now I wasn't initially going to include this factor, but it can sometimes work well to expedite the process of success, and it dovetails with time management, so here it is:

As the old saying goes, "a task fills the time available."

Have you ever noticed this? You have a project to do over the weekend and—voila!—you don't finish until Sunday night. It should have taken a couple hours, but instead it took the whole weekend. It's amazing how we waste time, how we fill it up with unnecessary tasks and distractions. So here is how we get a handle on this. You'll be glad you learned to tame this creature.

We employ this principle of *work fills space* to our own good. Shorten the time!

When you have a task, homework for example, take a moment to evaluate how much time each task will take. Make it tight, don't give yourself extra time—in fact, give yourself a little less than you think it requires. Then look at the clock and determine your checkpoints.

Math: About one minute per problem, thirty problems: Give yourself only 25 minutes. Watch the clock. Give yourself ten minutes for transition to the next subject. Use this time to get up stretch, get a glass of water or organize your next bit of work.

Science: 10 somewhat technical pages, maybe two or three minutes per page required. Give yourself only 20 or 25 minutes.

Write down the segments, put a time allotment next to each, and then add them for a total time.

A little pressure keeps you time aware, and keeps you from drifting off into unfocused effort. Of course, you need a reward for fulfilling this expedited session so be generous with yourself.

The intervening time between subjects can be used for task completion, if necessary, but you realize it comes out of your rest time, so try to work on schedule so *that* time is yours!

The key is to allot time for each assignment and then have an overall time frame for all of the homework combined. Keep an analog clock—round dial clock with the hands—in front of your workstation. Keep looking at it. Digital clocks don't give you the same feel for where you are relative to your goal. If you slip a little in one subject, you can then make it up in another, but if your overarching goal is, say, one hour total, then after one hour it's out to play or off to meet a friend.

Preview Materials

When I decided to make academic achievement a reality, I took a course in speed-reading. It wasn't magic, but I did take away some tricks—and they offer a few more tools for this project. I found speed-reading, used properly, improved both speed and comprehension—and could be applied to many subjects. I recommend such courses, but it's not a panacea. Here in a nutshell is what I learned.

First: If there are questions to be answered at the back of a chapter or section: read those before anything else.
Your mind will then be searching for answers, and enable a concentrated type of reading called active reading.

Second: Briefly skim the outline at the front, if there is one.

Then read the headings of each section and skim the first sentence or two of each. Most information in a section is contained in the first and last paragraph. This is true if you need to read the newspaper quickly as well. Read an article's first and last paragraph and you've probably acquired eighty-five percent of it.

You will now be able to read the text more quickly because you are reading with a goal in mind: To find the answers to the questions you found in the back of a chapter. Your mind will not be satisfied until it finds the answers, and it will be alert for them. *By reading the questions in advance,* you will have a better understanding of what is, or is not, important in the chapter.

Then go back and quickly skim the entire chapter, actively looking for the answers to the questions.

You can test this by doing one chapter the old fashioned way, reading the sections first then answering questions. Then compare it to the time and interest factor while doing the next chapter with this new system. I promise you will be pleasantly surprised how much easier and quicker this is.

Planning

Now I lay me down to sleep....

Another success factor is having a plan. Before bed each night, organize your following day. Create your list of priorities with the most critical items near the top of the list. Then enjoy the satisfaction of ticking them off as you go. Putting them down before you sleep frees your mind from having to worry over them. You'll sleep better too!

Procrastination

Procrastination is the bane of perfectionists. Many of us are guilty here. We want to do the job right—or more precisely...perfectly— so we wait until everything is aligned, until a block of time is available, the tasks of the day are less, and so on. Often this is never the case, and then something that must finally be done is done hurriedly at the last moment.

To avoid procrastination: break a task into little doable chunks. An example is cleaning out your desk and work area—another important thing. If you can't afford the time it requires to do a complete job, do a drawer a day. If you must tackle a sizeable subject, do it a section or chapter at a time, moving in a direction until your mind believes that you can indeed finish this most daunting task. The only words of wisdom I can offer here are:

A journey of a thousand miles begins with a single step

— Chinese proverb

STEP 7

Teacher Rapport

Look at the sky. We are not alone.
The whole universe is friendly to us
and conspires only to give the best
to those who dream and work.

—A. P. J. Abdul Kalam[10]

A student who shows interest is accorded more graces.

One of my engineering courses was Advanced Propulsion Systems. I was really concerned about this— I had no background in mechanics! At this point in time, all of my forays into auto mechanics were essentially failures. In trying to change a voltage regulator, I once accidentally touched a battery cable to the car frame and fried the whole electrical system. My humiliation was capped by having to have the car towed to a friend's garage to have the thing re-wired.

After the first day of class I asked the teacher for a few moments of his time to review my concerns and to find out what I could do to succeed in his course. This instructor had the reputation as the toughest professor in the aeronautics department. He was a brilliant man, reputed to have little patience for people who weren't. I discovered this was only partially true, he was brilliant but he was also patient and most encouraging.

He gave me the keys to what it would take to succeed in his class. I took notes and thanked him for his time. The pointers he gave me were less important than the few moments I took to solicit his help.

I learned that he had labeled me as an achiever, and he not only gave me high grades, but eventually placed me in charge of a group to rebuild an aircraft engine. My team was made up of the low academic achievers of the class, but to our good fortune they were very talented mechanics. We built the engine, and it ran beautifully. Unknown to me, at the time, this teacher had placed notes of very high praise in my academic files. I was grateful and learned that the first impressions you give to teachers can be the most important. They live to find students who want to learn what they have to teach. It validates who they are and to what they have dedicated their lives. So make an appointment early on with your teacher, and ask him or her how to succeed in class.

Some would contend that this is not playing fair. I would answer this with the response that soliciting your teacher's help is a life-skill. People like to be helpful, and helping students achieve success is frequently a teacher's life objective. They like to feel they've helped someone, and then they become invested in your success. Granted, my engineering course did not leave much room for subjective grading, but it smoothed out any problems that were sure to arise. So go ahead, make an appointment with your teachers, and find out what is critical to success in their class.

Do Extra Credit Work Whenever Offered!

Many teachers recognize that students don't all catch on to things the first time so they offer extra credit, or make-up tests to give another bite at the apple. Take advantage of this whenever possible. If nothing else, it shows you are motivated to succeed, and teachers will recognize your efforts in some manner.

Be a teacher, too!

I found that when I was a flight instructor, I learned a lot more about flying than when I was a student. Teaching informed me which mistakes are common, and what weaknesses give people the most trouble. I gained a more solid understanding of the material when I had to teach it. Consider offering to tutor someone in your class, or even a younger sibling. Besides giving you a direct benefit, it is a nice thing to do. While she took lessons, I asked my daughter to teach me the piano. She would learn a lesson, and then I asked her to show me what she had learned. We both benefited.

STEP 8

The Tricks

(Or: A Lifetime of Making Learning Fun!)

Any fool can know. The point is to understand.

— Albert Einstein

Memorizing

Using Association and Imagination

For those of us who are daydreamers, this is where it finally pays off. This is how learning becomes fun. How can that possibly be? The mind is like a powerful computer. It remembers everything —yes everything—you put into it. The retrieval system is what you have to develop because it is all in there, you just have to remember where you put it.

I suggest you find a good book on memorization. I recommend Harry Lorayne's Memory books.[11] They come in several varieties. Let me give you just the briefest examples of the most important elements of memorizing.

The first would be the imagination. You sometimes are required to take a rather dry subject and commit it to memory. The trick is to make it more imaginative.

You can easily memorize a long list of items in order by "linking"[12] one to the next with imaginative pictures. The secret is to exaggerate the picture in your mind, give it action and make it outrageous. If the words you are memorizing are difficult, find a meaning or sound they conjure in order to create a picture.

I offer an example here. Memorize these ten items with one read.

1. Rock
2. Boat
3. Saturn
4. Cloud
5. Temple

6. Nevada
7. Independence Day
8. Carpet
9. German Shepherd
10. Dress

Here is how you can quickly link these items. Use bold, out-of-proportion, large, action images in order to remember. If you have a good imagination—and what kid doesn't?—you will find it easy to memorize longs lists. Now, it's not only _okay_ to be silly, it is _essential_, and besides nobody is aware of these images except you, so have fun and they will stick.

Here goes my association. The first item is Rock. If you find it difficult to remember the first item, link it to yourself. Picture yourself reaching into your pocket and pulling out a large rock that becomes a huge rock—in other words, it couldn't have possibly fit in your pocket—or you could pull this big rock out of your ear. Use whatever works for you, just get a strong image in your mind.

I take the giant rock and heave it into a pool. It lands on a tiny <u>Boat</u>, which sinks under the water. It pops up and flies into space knocking into the rings of <u>Saturn</u>. The rings of Saturn begin to drop off sparkly dust, which forms into a Cloud over the earth. The cloud has lightning and thunder, and a bolt of lightning strikes a <u>Temple</u>—think action, loud and bright.

The temple flies up and lands in the state of <u>Nevada</u>—if you don't know the shape of Nevada, just picture it landing in the desert and turning into a giant slot machine, all lit up. Pull the handle on the slot machine—that was the Temple—and you see a line of "4's" appear in the windows. Then the machine begins shooting fireworks—think Fourth of July, <u>Independence Day.</u>

One of the fireworks lands on a <u>Carpet</u> which catches fire. Standing on the carpet is a <u>German Shepherd</u> dog wearing a <u>Dress</u>. He begins to jump up and down, as the carpet gets hot.

Now you can play those images back in your mind, having fixed them with one imaginative read, remembering them either backward or forward. If a word is difficult to remember, like prognosis, substitute a sound-a-like word, such as frog noses—picture frogs' noses. This should be close enough to allow your mind to associate the word prognosis with frog noses.

Keep the memorized list fresh in your mind by going over the associations from time to time.

As I said, get a good book on memorization techniques, like Harry Lorayne's, and use this to help you.

Mnemonics and Acronyms

Pneumonic. Sounds like a plague doesn't it? Well it is! But a mnemonic is a device or code. It is the formation of a word or phrase that is made up from the first letters of a sequence, which you are trying to remember. Now a mnemonic is a good learning tool, but imagination and linking are generally better, yet at times it is best to use them together!

Acronyms

An acronym is a word formed from the initial letter of each successive part, like FBI, which of course stands for
Federal
Bureau of
Investigation

Another example, to remember the names of the Great Lakes just remember the acronym:

Homes
Huron
Ontario
Michigan
Erie
Superior

Mnemonics

A mnemonic is a short phrase that helps you remember something.

Formulas are sometimes a good use of mnemonics. To remember the basic trigonometric equations just remember:

<u>S</u>ome <u>O</u>ld <u>H</u>orses <u>C</u>an <u>A</u>lways <u>H</u>ear <u>T</u>heir <u>O</u>wners <u>A</u>pproach.

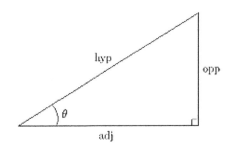

Sine	=	Opposite/Hypotenuse
Cosine	=	Adjacent/Hypotenuse
Tangent	=	Opposite/Adjacent

Make up your own, and make them funny and lively!

Power Learning™:
The Secret Weapon in Ultra Academics

One of my best secrets to learning effectively is something I call *Power Learning*™.

It is so simple, yet so powerfully effective that you might discount the whole idea, but I strongly suggest you give it serious consideration.

One of the things I didn't mention is that while in college, I worked in a job both before and after school as I concurrently acquired flight training *and* achieved nearly straight A's; I was also in the best shape of my life. Being an A-student does not mean being a pencil-necked geek. I discovered, quite by accident, exercising while studying actually made me smarter!

Eventually I incorporated exercise into my study routine. Typically, I would prepare my study/homework session by (as you will recall) figuring out how long each subject would take, and then allot the right amount of time. I would then break down each subject—say physics—into sub-elements, pages or sections. At the conclusion of each section of questions or paragraphs, I would perform a workout routine—something like fifty pushups, or one hundred jumping jacks. I would still go to the gym three days each week, but this interim exercise supplemented my health regimen while keeping my blood flowing for the study session.

If I neglected my workout I found my mind wandering and my focus fading. When I used this method, the oxygen to my brain kept me easily on focus and I retained the information better.

This is particularly important for younger children. They are meant to play and move around. Confining them to a desk or chair for hours of study is cruel and unhealthful, and, fortunately, totally unnecessary. When I would do homework with my children and see them begin to fade, I would pretend to be a drill sergeant and have them drop and give me ten pushups or twenty jumping jacks. It was a game we played. At first they would pretend to balk, so I would add five or ten more. We made it fun, and they knew not to protest too much or their labors would be doubled! Sometimes when they'd feel they needed more movement, they would pretend to argue, and so they'd get to do even more exercise, which they found invigorating. It was a great break from the occasional monotony of study, and great fun—I truly miss those moments.

Long after those wonderful joint homework sessions, I would sometimes see my son get up from doing his homework at the kitchen table and drop down for ten pushups without anyone saying a word. He appreciates the value of this concept and his grades reflect it. My eldest daughter didn't always think this was so cool, but I would still see her get up and stretch or take a brief walk or shoot some baskets between her studies because she realized that sitting too long is neither healthy nor productive.

On this subject, it is also beneficial to start your day with some brisk aerobics or a workout. When you exercise, the endorphins and increased blood flow to the brain oxygenate it, thus, enhancing not only your thinking ability, but also your outlook. When you organize your day to incorporate morning exercises, the benefits will be manifold.

Dance your way to A's

If you prefer, put on some music and dance around the
room. Beware; your roommates may not understand
the value of this—you may want to close the door before
you rock out. The beauty of this technique is that the
aerobic benefit could also be one of your little rewards
for finishing a section of work. Who doesn't like to
dance? And yes, I actually still do this from time to time
in my hotel room when I'm working.

Take a Walk

Another technique to enhance learning is to take a walk,
stopping at short intervals and memorizing some fact
and then associating it with a point on your stroll—a
bench, a big rock, something memorable. Then during a
test, you just mentally re-walk the course, retrieving the
relevant data as you go. The walk is aerobic and the
associations are easier because they are concrete and
retrievable. If you cannot walk outside, just walk around
a familiar room, associating as you move methodically
in one direction around the room.

Of course this method is more effective when using the
techniques already discussed. The item to memorize
should be memorable—that is, make it out of the
ordinary, with movement, change its size or alter its
color. Make it oddly memorable as we discussed above.
The method of linking as described above is probably
more accessible and can be honed to a usable skill, but
walking is very pleasant so why not use this method
once in a while as well. The technique, called the
"method of loci" was purportedly invented by a Greek
poet named Simonides of Ceos. The ancient Greek
orators had to memorize great quantities of information

in their speeches and poetry. They could not write it down and had to keep it all organized in their heads. Why not try a technique that's been in use for thousands of years?

Different Subjects Require Slightly Different Approaches

Math

Try to step back and look at the big picture of a section. Try to find the application in real life. I saw my daughter struggle with this at times, as I did at a young age, because she didn't take an extra moment to figure out just "where is this knowledge leading, what's in it for me? How does this apply to my life? Who the heck uses this stuff and why?

These are simple questions, but once answered they make math more meaningful and memorable. Please bear with me while I tell you a story. Stories are great learning tools, no?

One evening my daughter was tasked with finding the mathematical areas of various odd shapes. She was trying to merely grab for formulas she had learned rather than taking a brief moment to just recognize relationships.

The figures were squares and rectangles with half circles, like arched windows or hour glasses in a square. My first question to her was, "What do you recognize? Is anything familiar to you?" Like all kids, she jumped to the easy answer, "No!"

"Come on now, what does this shape remind you of?"

"A window?"

"Now we're getting somewhere." Relating to *your* life is a key to understanding.

"What is the area of *your* window?"

"I don't know?" Again, the *kid* answer... and I'm not filling the blanks in that easily for her.

"So let's go over here to your window and now you tell me: what is the area of your window?"

"What shape is it?"

"You tell me!"

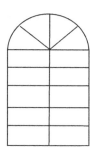

Kids are masters of getting information from you, but they doubt their own observations. Allow them to draw their own conclusions and then act upon them. Take this concept into your own life. Try to figure stuff out! It is very empowering.

My daughter continues, "Okay, it looks like a rectangle here."

"Yes, very good...so what's the area?"

"How tall is it?"

"For now just give it a round number in say feet," I add helpfully.

"Okay, five feet tall."

"Yes." She's waiting for me to jump in and take over the problem. I resist the urge.

"And it's about four feet wide."

"Okay." No commitment here.

"So, where is the length? I know the width, but is tall the same as length?"

Bingo! "What do you think?" Now there is relationship, and hence understanding.

"Yes, I multiply these two to find the area."

"Great job, you figured it out."

"But what about this round part here?"

"Okay, what about it?"

> Kids are like attorneys examining a witness. They offer leading question hoping you will fill in all of the particulars. I admit, sometimes I bite and begin my explanations, but I aspire to draw out the answers making the exercise more meaningful. They listen more when *they* are talking.

"What shape is it?"

"You tell me." Oh no I don't.

"What does it look like?" I offer encouragingly.

"It looks like half of a circle"

"Yes it does."

"I don't know the formula for half a circle."

"What do you know the formula for?"

"I know the formula for a circle"

"Okay." Pause.

Longer pause from her. She's beating me. I'm bursting to tell her the answer, but again I probe her mind.

"What is the formula for the area of a circle?"

"Pi r-squared," she recites dutifully.

"Do we know any of those components?"

"I know pi."

"Well, how about r?"

"Well r is measured from the middle of the circle to the edge, but where is the middle?"

"Well if you pictured the whole circle on top of this window, where would you place it?"

Quickly she says, "It would go here."

"Yes, so from where would you measure *r*?"

"From right here."

"And what is that measurement, roughly?"

"Well it looks like about two feet."

"Okay, how did you figure that?"

"Well the window is four feet wide, and that's about half way."

$$A = \pi \, r^2$$

"Oh, so you're saying that the radius of this circle we've plopped on here is equal to half of the width of this rectangle here?" Just trying to summarize her observations and put them in relatable terms.

"Yes."

"So what is the area?"

"Pi times r-squared, *r* is two, so *r*-squared is four, so it's four-pi."

"Yes, but that's for the whole circle, isn't it?"

"Oh, yes, we need only half."

"Yes..." *Bite tongue. Do not answer.*

"How do I get half?" she asks, but the answer lies in her question, so I continue to bite my tongue.

"Do I divide by two?"

"Viola! And that answer would be...?"

"Two-pi."

"It all makes sense doesn't it? Well done!"

"Now, did we answer the question?"

"What was the question?" This is what kids do. They lose the big picture, while working on the components.

Now is my opportunity to give her a study skill, "When you complete a problem, look back at the question to see if you answered it—completely! My question was: What is the area of your window."

"Well I guess I have to add the two together, is that right?"

"What do you think?" Ever the inscrutable master, I don't wish to rob her of her own victory.

"Yes, I'll add the rectangle plus the half circle area."

"Excellent, *always check back to the question to be certain you answered all of it.* Well done!"

We do one more problem to solidify her thinking, but the major point is, my daughter needed to relate the little figures and formulas in her book to her life, and she needed to borrow from her usual practices of dividing things in half in order to hitch the information.

As parents we must learn well the phrase, "What do you think?" Why confine this perspective to parenting and bring this question to our own life. How does this work? What do I know about things that apply to this? What do I think?

Math has unfortunately gained a dark mystique. It has become accepted that some people are good at math, while others aren't math people. To some degree this is true, but I think a good measure can be attributed to one's exposure. If you are introduced to math in a fun and meaningful way, it becomes fun and meaningful.

Did you ever hear your parents or an older sibling say, "Math is hard", or "I never did get math," or other such negative comments, because that reality may become *yours* unless you actively challenge and reject such negativity in your own life, which may rob you of opportunities., If you ever hear your inner voice saying such things, replace them immediately with more positive ones. I did this, and my math grades went from average to A's.

When doing math, find a relationship with your life. Use shapes of things you know, measurements for everyday use, formulas that will work for you, applications in the real world—*your world.* If this isn't apparent, ask your teacher how a particular element of math is applicable, what is this used for? Teachers sometimes forget to relate these things to real life. It helps. It also *sticks* for your lifetime and you can use math to solve your daily problems—figure out change, determine the height of a building or calculate how much paper you'll need to cover twenty picnic tables. In my own life I use the concepts of trigonometry to quickly figure out crosswinds and tailwinds as I taxi to the end of the runway. It's not difficult. It just takes a little thought once in a while to ask myself, how can I do this?

A short story. *You need the break after the math example, don't you?* I was sitting in the waiting room of my dentist one day when I was much younger. A mother came in with her two children. The children, like most bright kids, were asking a lot of questions. The mother, bless her, was the most patient person I had ever seen. She never batted their questions away, instead, she asked them to examine the answer in the context of what they already knew. She did this not once, but several times while we sat in the waiting room. I knew these kids were going to grow up to be amazingly capable. They were barely grade school students, yet already they were expert at critical thinking. At that moment I made a promise to myself that I would always try to figure things out, and, if I ever had kids, I would do exactly as this fantastic woman did. I would allow them to figure things out for themselves too...and you know what, it worked!

Let's figure it out

Reading

Refer to section *Preview Materials* under Step 6. In addition to previewing the material, reading the questions at the end, reading the sections headings, you should be certain that you are in a quiet environment. Find a place where you won't be interrupted. Be certain to have good light over your shoulder, a place with no glare, and make sure that your posture is comfortable.

If reading causes you difficulty, I would recommend you take one of the many speed and comprehension courses. It might be possible to borrow them from your public library.

There are some mechanical elements to effective speed-reading. One of the important techniques is to read groups of words instead of individual words. A method that helps facilitate this is to move your finger down the page in a steady motion and following behind, read entire lines with your eyes. This takes some learning. You may wish to start by beginning your reading at say the third or fourth word in from the left. Try to read words in clumps rather than as individual words. An alternative is to move your fingers and eyes in a Z pattern reading above your fingers as you move them down the page. This forces you to move quickly, without stopping or fixating as we are inclined to do if we read less thoughtfully.

The other important technique to speed-read is to quiet the inner voice in your head that reads or narrates as you move along. This limits our speed. So you must work to actively squash it. I try to do this by out-reading it. Sometimes I slow down and I can hear it again, so I make a conscious effort to speed-read when necessary to quiet the inner voice and breeze along.
In speed-reading, we move along in a continuous motion, which causes us to miss words. These words are generally not important. Our mind should furnish the important missing pieces by contextually considering the adjoining text. The important thing is to not go back and re-read sections where we dropped words. If they are important, they will be reemphasized further down.

Comprehension is improved through the methods outlined in Step 6 above. These include pre-screening the materials by reading any questions at the back of a section *first*. Your mind will then be actively reading. That is, your mind will be actively looking for the answers that lie in the questions to follow. This will keep you focused and engaged, like hunting for Easter eggs. [Do you see how I repeated this point? It is important!]

Skimming the paragraph titles and subtitles before you begin to read allows you to have a little preview of where this reading will be taking you and the basic road markers along the way.

To summarize, the essential elements of speed-reading are:

1. Read the questions at the back of a section first to foster active reading.
2. Skim the table of contents, and then review the paragraph titles and sub-titles so your mind has a map.
3. Suppress your inner voice.
4. Use a mechanical method to move down the page such as reading in groups of words and chunks of sections in lieu of individual words.
5. Do not re-read to fill in the missing words. Let your mind fill in the pieces.

Note: Sometimes speed-reading is not the appropriate method to acquire the information you need. Sometimes, you must indeed focus on every word or re-read for full understanding, as when reading poetry or literature. Sometimes it is important to read for language. You will have to be the judge. You may still benefit, however, from the concepts used in speed-reading for faster acquisition of the information at hand.

Writing

Now here is an area where many students have difficulty. In order to be a good writer, you must be a good—and prolific—reader. Read *good* books. A starting point is with a list of the classics. A good librarian can help you here, or perhaps you can do an online search. Reading tons of comic books or poorly written newspapers—so many are poorly written— won't make you a good writer. Good books make good writers. Simple, isn't it?

Become familiar with a thesaurus. They are easily searchable online. These offer a rich variety of word choices, so you can expertly express yourself. There are also several great vocabulary books. If you wish to build a strong ability to speak and write, you should look into getting a copy for your own library. I have found learning new words to be a fine hobby. It has paid handsomely, as you are judged by the words you use. Your paycheck may depend upon it.

> I once read an article about how Jack Welch, the vaunted former chairman of General Electric, chose his successor. He was considering a successful insider of many years until this man misused a word. He said that someone of his stature should know how to use the language, or people will be hesitant to follow his lead. Do you need a more powerful statement for learning words and their proper use than this?

When writing, consider doing several drafts, at least two. Place the work aside for a day or two and then revisit it with a fresh eye to make corrections. Your rough draft will be a time for inspiration, let it flow, without the encumbrance of worry for grammar, spelling or punctuation; that's the function of the second reading, or draft.

When you find a voice you like, a favorite author, try to read as much of their work as possible, and then adopt some of their style. I have found books on speeches to be a powerful way to learn the most effective oratorical and writing skills. One of my favorites is by a man for whom English was a second language: the great American Indian warrior, Red Jacket. Now here was a man who understood that war would soon be an anachronism, so he adopted the newer, more powerful weapon: speech.[13]

STEP 9

Nutrition and Health:
Eating your way to achievement

One cannot think well, love well, sleep well,
if one has not dined well

—Virginia Woolf[14]

Food

Eat breakfast but only if you want to be smart! Our brains and bodies need fuel; if they don't get it they start to shut down less vital processes, like high-level thinking. The body and brain begin to slow down to conserve.

Even the U.S. Government recognizes the correlation between good nutrition and learning, as exemplified by the breakfast and lunch programs now in place at schools across the country. Studies determined that children, who did not have proper nutrition, particularly breakfast, were falling behind their peers in class. We are still failing our children in the quality of food we serve them at schools. When one sees the food served in French schools, it is easy to see we come up short. Their meals are freshly prepared and well-balanced. We still have a ways to go here, but my hope is that if you are old enough to read this, you are thoughtful enough to eat healthful meals. We should at least appreciate this by not skipping breakfast, because, if we do, we are cheating our brains, and jeopardizing our prospects in life—is this clear enough!?[15]

I am not a nutrition expert, but after reviewing those who are, I have come up with a few suggestions. For a deeper understanding of how food affects the brain, please refer to the endnotes.

Eat lightly before tests. A heavy meal will take the blood away from your brain. Avoid processed sugar before a test. It will bring you up, and then drop you even lower before the test is over. Fruits, like oranges and apples, are a good way to pep you up without creating too much of a sugar rush.

The most important thing to remember is this, eat a balanced diet. Don't skip meals.

There are a few vitamins and minerals that are touted as *brain foods*, but one that has shown to have real capability and power seems to be choline.[16] [17]

How? Choline is a building block, a precursor to acetylcholine, a chemical which allows the nerve endings to fire more rapidly.

One study demonstrated that a pregnant rat given choline had offspring with better learning abilities later in life than rats that had no choline. It's not too late for us!

Studies indicate it may protect the liver, too, by flushing a cholesterol carrier out of the organ and allowing the body to rid itself of homocysteine[18] as well. Studies showed that people given choline actually reversed their liver damage.

Choline rich foods: Calves liver, Egg yolks, skim milk, soybean seeds (lecithin), lentils.

Powdered lecithin supplements are available from the health food store that can be spread on cereal, ice cream or in a fruit smoothie.

Many other foods have purported brain-enhancing capabilities. You can look into this on your own, but do be aware there also are foods that are bad for your brain. Processed sugars aren't good. Especially avoid them when performing tests. A natural alternative is fruit. This has the benefits, without the deleterious effects. A little fruit just before a test may be the perfect pick-me-up you need. If you are nervous, perhaps you might try a banana. It has potassium[19]—a muscle-relaxer—and   tryptophan –an essential amino acid that among many benefits increases serotonin when administered orally in a purified form. Serotonin has been found to reduce aggression and increase agreeableness. Who doesn't want that?[20]

Calcium, along with zinc and magnesium, has been shown to keep you calm, if that's what you need. B vitamins are good for keeping you generally energized and allowing your organs to function well under stress. A regular dose of a good B complex is critical to energy, along with D3 for keeping afternoon fatigue away. If you want a pick-me-up vitamin, try the occasional sub-lingual vitamin B12 tab when you feel yourself fading. You can occasionally take this alone but a balanced B vitamin (B-Complex) will avoid the deleterious effects of over emphasis on one B vitamin, [21] which can undermine other vitamins. The sub-lingual tab is fast-acting.

Sleep

Students are generally still growing and require more sleep than adults—eight hours isn't enough for young people. Athletes in training need more sleep to repair their bodies. So make sure to get proper sleep, and be particularly well rested at test time. Forego late-night cram sessions or favorite TV shows. Use TV shows and such as rewards when the tests are over.

There are several methods to induce sleep quickly, we won't go too deeply into them here, but suffice to say that you should not take your work to bed with you.

Take a pen and paper to outline your tasks for tomorrow before you go to bed. This will not only afford you an expedient way to handle forthcoming tasks, but it will also free your mind. You won't have to worry about forgetting something—it will be available to you in the morning!

Use the last few minutes to let your mind relax with *other* things, a good book, some relaxing music, meditation, or prayer. Reflect at bedtime, because it gives one a last chance to focus on what's important—to keep things in perspective.

STEP 10

Test-Taking

Do not rely completely on any other human being, however dear.
We meet all life's greatest tests alone.

—Agnes Macphail[22]

Test-taking is as much art as skill. If you have studied
and prepared properly, a test should *not* be a nerve-
wracking experience, but an opportunity to show off a
bit.

Learn the Material

As we've discussed, the brain is a powerful mechanism.
It is more powerful than any super-computer built to
date—but you knew that. One of the amazing things it
can do is adjust and remember. I discovered this while
teaching pilots at our airline. One of the courses I
taught took three days. On day one students would
commonly have some difficulty making the simulator fly
as they wished. Their inputs were jerky, and they had
trouble maintaining the basic instrument flight must-
haves: heading, altitude and airspeed. But on day two,
miraculously the thing would fly like a dream. I can only
attribute this to the brain's ability to recalibrate
overnight. What an amazing and powerful thing our
brain is if one stops to consider it.

Use this fact to your advantage. If you use flashcards to
prepare for a test, or if you use the memorization
techniques touched on earlier—and sometimes a

combination works well where you make up a flashcard that stimulates your memory of the linking of ideas—you can use the following method. Three days before the test, go through the cards and memory items before bed. The day before the test in the morning go over the items to be remembered. If you find something you get stuck on, highlight it—perhaps in yellow. Then the night before the test, go over the items one more time. If again you find a few sticky points, highlight them in a bold color like pink—these will be the items you give extra attention to in the morning.

Finally, on test <u>morning, zip through your memorization, or flashcards, touching only on the subjects with the bold highlights. This is a bit of overkill, a three day prep, but this will ensure a top grade and a thorough understanding—that's the point here, right?</u>

Mental Preparation

If you are confident in the material, this next part is fun and easy. Go through your affirmations (see STEP 5), and perhaps make up one or two just for the upcoming test. The affirmation could be something like: *I am relaxed and happy to take this test, to show what I've learned, or my mind is clear and the information I need comes to me easily. I am enjoying this test, because I am relaxed and prepared.*

Now visualize yourself in the actual classroom in which you will take the test. See the room, smell the wooden desks, feel it in your imagination with your hands. Picture yourself sitting there relaxed, just humming away with ready answers as the test proceeds, effortlessly plucking from your mind the information needed and placing it on paper. You are actually happy, because the test is so easy, and you are finishing it so quickly. Don't forget to repeat these just as you sit for the exam.

If you have the ability, a short meditation just prior to entering the test is most helpful. If you don't have that, stop for a moment and take three slow, deep breaths. A quiet, calming moment before entering the arena—it really works.

Taking the Test

You've most likely heard these before, but at this point they're worth repeating. As you take the test, be aware of the time. Take a quick scan to see how long the thing will take, and, as you do with your homework, give yourself an estimate. Then keep pace as you go. With all of your preparation, you'll probably find it going fast.

If you get stuck on a problem, make a small pencil mark in the margin. Be careful with this on scanned test forms because the mark could affect the grading, and be sure to erase the marks. They needn't be too dark if they are all in the same section of the margin, just dark enough for your eyes to return to the problem. I use a small circle to be checked through when a problem is complete, and only a small mark for problems that could possibly benefit from one more review, such as long problems, which are ripe for one tiny mistake. By skipping the problem, after briefly attempting it, your brain will work on it at the subconscious level—sounds farfetched, but it's true. While you are busy doing the easier problems, it is solving the one you were stuck on. It's the same dynamic as brain self-calibration discussed previously. You may liken it to today's multi-core computer processors.

At the end of the test, come back and address the problems you didn't finish, or those you found difficult. You will be amazed that your subconscious has gained further insight in the interim. Don't forget to mark the ones that are challenging, too, even if you thought you got them right, as a quick check can sometimes reveal a step or two you've missed. Let's say you use two dots or two circles for a missed problem, ones you couldn't get on the first go, or say you skipped problems, and use one circle for a challenging problem you'd like to revisit if you have the time. Do whatever works for you, but it is important to be consistent. This system will prioritize the problems for you.

At the conclusion of the test, go over the marked problems. Attack the missed and unfinished problems first, followed by the challenging ones. Then—and this is what separates the A's from the B's—review *all* of the problems, either beginning at the top, or for a different perspective start at the bottom and work backward. This little exercise can sometimes catch a mistake or two, which could mean a grade level. This will help you utilize the whole time effectively, even if it means some repetition. Remember to set a reward for after the test—you deserve it, you've done good work!

You've heard before that in a multiple-choice test, the longest answer is often the right one because in order to make it the correct choice, it requires a more detailed description, hence its length. If this doesn't help, conventional wisdom says to pick answer C, because teachers like to throw the curves first then bury the real answer. If it comes down to it, rely on these tricks, but hopefully it won't be necessary if you are using these techniques.

On multiple-choice tests, it is best to grab the answer you think of first, and then eliminate the others one by one. Sometimes an answer will have a tiny flaw, which another answer does not: pick the *best* answer. The only way to ensure what is best is to *review all of the choices before moving on.*

The next issue to consider is elimination. Mark each choice in a problem that isn't correct, leaving you with perhaps one or two remaining possible answers. Which one has a disqualifying element? Which one sounds *most* correct?

If in doubt, your first impression is usually correct.

An aside here, I once had a history professor whose final was only true and false questions. All correct answers were false. This was not a good learning experience, and he was not a good teacher.

So another caveat, figure out your teacher. If he is a grump, maybe more answers are false than not. Here is a more important life lesson, on rare occasions you may have to speak to the dean about such behavior. There are a few professors—very, very few— who have forgotten why they went into teaching, or who have some personal dilemma present in their life. Learn to recognize these types. I understand that it's not easy. The first course of action is to approach the teacher and try to work it out. Do not be intimidated, but do be friendly and have your argument thoughtfully organized. If that is unsuccessful, you could at the very least with the help of the dean have the class reduced to a pass-fail grade and thereby protect your GPA—

everything is negotiable: another life skill that will serve you well.

The funny thing is—and I can laugh at this now—one student in this odd history class butted heads with this guy all through the semester. He was only there half the time anyway. The teacher had personal issues, and a lot of negativity that he brought to the class, and this student would have no part of it. Watching this dynamic of confrontation with a teacher was an eye-opener for me, I was a mere first semester freshman. When the final came, this student grabbed the test, marked all of the answers false and defiantly threw it down on the teacher's desk in about two minutes. I sat there fascinated. I'd been groomed in parochial schools where you never went up against the teacher.

I do not advocate confrontation with a teacher. My experience has been that they are generally wonderful people who really care about your success. They are also generally intelligent and sufficiently self-aware to accept where they've fallen down if it is presented in a mature, non-confrontational and help-seeking manner. Oddly, this recalcitrant student was the only one to get an "A" in the course. Because the final was a heavily weighted part of the grade and he correctly marked all of the answers false. Really? This test had no learning value. Here's another lesson: life isn't always fair...but that's a subject for another book.

Test-Taking Summary:

1. Learn and review the material in the days leading to the exam.
2. Make affirmations, repeating those days before, and just prior to, exam.
3. Meditate to summon calmness just prior to test. Minimally, take a few deep breaths.
4. Mark in test margin unfinished and more challenging problems for review.
5. Use elimination to disqualify wrong answers.
6. If that fails, longest answers in multiple-choice problems are often correct.
7. Choice C is often the right answer.
8. First impressions are usually correct.

A last note...

In college you learn more than numbers and figures. You learn to negotiate the world. Real people work with people, and as I learned from my next door neighbor fresh out of college, *everything is negotiable.* Teach your kids that it is possible to reason with teachers—*of course*—only after they have put in the work. I encouraged mine to present a reasoned argument. That is, go to the teacher with facts and figures. Prepare your case as if you were in court. This doesn't always work, but what have you got to lose?

Teachers are human (no really!). They appreciate someone with ambition, drive and presence. If you enter their office arguing—whether you are right or wrong—you may, in fact, lose. But if you go in with the intention to demonstrate to the teacher that this grade is important to you and your future, and that, yes, you understand the material, perhaps there was some misunderstanding involved, but, if you consider *this* work, consider your participation and effort and *this* earlier paper for which full credit was not received, well, then maybe he or she would consider re-evaluating your grade.

If that goes well—or doesn't—be gracious, and thank them for having taken a moment to listen to you. This skill may be more important than achieving perfect grades, as it will serve you for the rest of your life. Remember, teachers are people, good people. Listen to their insights. Be honest, forthright and appreciative— they deserve it!

Conclusion

Review this book from time to time. You may find information you haven't fully utilized for a while.

Find your motivation to succeed. Take a serious and thoughtful time to find this motivation. Then go ahead, set your goals. Use the outline as a guide to keep you on track in your studies.

Work smart by working fast. Your reward—for a job well done of course—is to enjoy the down time. When I procrastinated, in my youth, I could never really enjoy the time I had, because it felt stolen. When completing my tasks quickly and efficiently, my free time was indeed *free*.

I wish for you all the abundance I've enjoyed from finding theses few precious secrets...

...now go set the world on fire!

After Words

I should note that it took me a while to figure out how to achieve A's. I was motivated, but I hadn't honed the tools. But by the time I reached my final academic years I had it down pretty well. I never formalized my approach until the first iteration of this book, but I tried to teach my children the value of these methods along the way. They have all exceeded my deepest aspirations for them—and far surpassed me! I could not be more proud!

I'm proud of you too for having made it to the end of this book. You must have already found some of your motivation—keep pursuing that. Observation, examination and critical thinking are the foundations of intellectual growth. Intellect is that which moves all of us forward.

Now, I ask of you what I always ask of my children— *please make the world a better place.*

> *Whatever you are by nature, keep to it;*
> *never desert your own line of talent.*
> *Be what nature intended you for and you will succeed;*
> *be anything else,*
> *and you will be ten thousand times worse than nothing.*
>
> — Sydney Smith[23]

Endnotes

---

[1] "Eleanor Roosevelt." First Lady. Though not found in any of her original writings, this quote was noted in the biography, *It Seems to Me : Selected Letters of Eleanor Roosevelt* (2001) by Leonard C. Schlup and Donald W. Whisenhunt

[2] "Mahatma Gandhi." Quote attributed to Mahatma Gandhi. Earlier versions exist in essentially the same form dating to Isidore of Seville. Reputed to derive from his *Etymologiae*, an etymological encyclopedia containing a compilation of extracts of myriad books from classical antiquity imperiled by the onset of the Dark Ages, a time of economic and cultural degeneration commencing in the 5th century. The same message is also attributed to Muhammad via the Hadith (حاديث, *'aḥādīṯ*): a collection of the reports claiming to quote what the prophet Muhammad said verbatim on any matter.

[3] The university has since returned to the Latin system of distinction. Graduation with Great Distinction would now be the equivalent of Summa Cum Laude

[4] "Norman Ralph Augustine." One of America's most dedicated public servants. Among his many notable contributions, he has served as Undersecretary to the Army, former CEO Lockheed Martin, and Professor at Princeton University. Presented the National Medal of Technology, and five time recipient of the Department of Defense's highest civilian decoration, the Distinguished Civilian Service Award.

[5] "Ralph Marston." Ralph Marston - GreatDay.com. Inspirational motivator dedicated to helping people realize their own value and potential. Lives in Austin, TX.

[6] Patricia Harkness. Harkness, Patricia Sampson, and Richard C. Lombard. *What If the Glass Breaks: Life of a Disability Activist : The Bob Sampson Story*. Denver: Outskirts, 2013. Print.

[7] http://german.about.com/library/blgermyth12.htm
The following academic review of this quote comes from the About.com German Language Website.

"The... quotation often attributed to Goethe is in fact by William Hutchinson Murray (1913-1996), from his 1951 book entitled The Scottish Himalayan Expedition. The actual final lines from W.H. Murray's book
  Whatever you can do, or dream you can do, begin it.
  Boldness has genius, power, and magic in it!"

[8] Excerpt(s) from JITTERBUG PERFUME by Tom Robbins, 1985 by Tom Robbins. Used by permission of Bantam Books, an imprint of Random House, a division of Penguin Random House LLC, All rights reserved. Any third party use of this material, outside of this publication, is prohibited. Interested parties must apply directly to Penguin Random House LLC for permission.

[9] John Randolph (1773-1833), U.S. congressman and senator from Virginia, serving at various times between 1799 and 1833. He was deemed brilliant by both enemies and friends for his rapier wit and oratory skills. Ultimately his giftedness was overcome by madness, believed to be a consequence of tuberculosis, which eventually claimed his life. He gave us many notable quotations, including, "A state can no more give up part of her sovereignty than a lady can give up part of her virtue."

[10] A.P. J. Abdul Kalam, (1931-2015), 11th President of India. Affectionately known as the 'people's president.' Served only one term before returning to his profession as an aerospace scientist. He came close to realizing his dream of becoming a fighter pilot, but placed ninth in qualifying for only eight positions in the Indian Air Force. In addition to rocket science, and numerous advanced engineering projects, he also is credited with medical inventions including a low cost heart stent.

[11] Lorayne, Harry. *Super Memory--super Student: How to Raise Your Grades in 30 Days*. Boston: Little, Brown, 1990. Print.

[12] "Linking" is the term used by Harry Lorayne in his memory programs.

[13] Indian Warrior Chief, Red Jacket to the council of chiefs of the Six Nations in 1805 after a white missionary had addressed them. Copeland, Lewis, and Lawrence W. Lamm. *The World's Great Speeches*. 3rd Enl. ed. New York: Dover Publications, 1973. Print.

[14] Adeline Virginia Woolf (1882-1941), who wrote under the name of Virginia Woolf, was a modernist English writer; educated at home by highly literate parents in London, later taking courses at Kings College! She lent her voice to the nascence of feminism.

[15] http://www.ncbi.nlm.nih.gov/books/NBK20414/

http://www.foodforthebrain.org/smart-kids
http://www.pcrm.org/shop/byNealBarnard/power-foods-for-the-brain
http://www.ncbi.nlm.nih.gov/pubmed/15640516
http://www.berkeleywellness.com/supplements/vitamins/article/should-you-boost-your-choline

[16] http://www.ncbi.nlm.nih.gov/pubmed/15640516

[17] http://www.berkeleywellness.com/supplements/vitamins/article/should-you-boost-your-choline

[18] Hyperhomocysteinemia has been correlated with the occurrence of blood clots, heart attacks and strokes, though it is unclear whether hyperhomocysteinemia is an independent risk factor for these conditions. Hyperhomoscyteinemia has also been associated with early pregnancy loss.

http://en.wikipedia.org/wiki/Homocysteine,
http://www.ncbi.nlm.nih.gov/pubmed/12871504

[19] Significance
Potassium plays a vital role in normal nerve and muscle function. A low potassium level inhibits muscle relaxation, causing rigid muscles that lead to tension and impaired function. Common symptoms of a potassium deficiency include muscle weakness and spasms, and if left untreated, potassium deficiency can cause the breakdown of muscle tissue, a condition known as rhabdomyolysis. The Institute of Medicine recommends that adults consume 4,700 mg of potassium per day to support muscle function, keep the heart beating rhythmically and maintain a healthy blood pressure. http://www.livestrong.com/article/493009-what-role-does-potassium-play-in-muscle-contraction/

[20] Young SN (2013). "The effect of raising and lowering tryptophan levels on human mood and social behaviour". Philos. Trans. R. Soc. Lond., B, Biol. Sci. 368 (1615): 20110375. doi:10.1098/rstb.2011.0375. PMC 3638380. PMID 23440461.

[21] Too much B6 can cause nerve damage. A balanced B complex ameliorates this. Foca FJ (September 1985). "Motor and sensory neuropathy secondary to excessive pyridoxine ingestion". Arch Phys Med Rehabil. 66 (9): 634–6. PMID 2994596.

[22] Agnes Campbell Macphail (McPhail) (1890-1954) Canadian politician and first woman elected to parliament. She was elected to the House of Commons from 1921 to 1940, and responsible for Ontario's first equal-pay legislation, as well as workers' rights as a progressive Canadian politician.

[23] Sydney Smith (1771-1845), Essayist and Anglican cleric.
English humorist, writer and Anglican cleric. Took a degree in 1792 from New College, Oxford and a Master of Arts degree in 1796. He intended to read for the bar, but as a consequence of influences from his father was ordained at Oxford in 1796. He lectured on moral philosophy at the Royal Institution. His progressive lectures favored the education of women, the abolition of slavery and advocated the teaching of practical subjects in lieu of the classics.

About the Author

Brian Atchison is the proud father of three magnificent children with whom he has shared the secrets of this book. He is a Boeing 777 captain and training pilot for a major international airline based in San Francisco. He tries to convince his children that he is responsible for the iPhone, because he once pulled Apple co-founder Steve Wozniak out of an airplane crash—they remain dubious. He lives at Lake Tahoe.

Made in United States
Orlando, FL
27 December 2022